RAFAEL PALMEIRO

A Real-Life Reader Biography

Barbara Marvis

Mitchell Lane Publishers, Inc.
P.O. Box 200 • Childs, Maryland 21916

jB 10/98
cop.1

Mitchell Lane
PUBLISHERS

First Printing

Real-Life Reader Biographies

Selena	Robert Rodriguez	Mariah Carey	**Rafael Palmeiro**
Tommy Nuñez	Trent Dimas	Cristina Saralegui	Andres Galarraga
Oscar De La Hoya	Gloria Estefan	Jimmy Smits	Mary Joe Fernandez
Cesar Chavez	Isabel Allende	Carlos Mencia	Jaime Escalante

Library of Congress Cataloging-in-Publication Data
Marvis, Barbara J.
    Rafael Palmeiro / Barbara Marvis.
      p. cm. — (A real-life reader biography)
    Includes index.
    Summary: Presents a biography emphasizing the career of the talented first baseman for the Baltimore Orioles.
    ISBN 1-883845-49-1 (lib. bdg.)
    1. Palmeiro, Rafael, 1964– —Juvenile literature. 2. Baseball players—Cuba—Biography—Juvenile literature. [1.
Palmeiro, Rafael, 1964– . 2. Baseball players. 3. Cuban Americans—Biography.] I. Title. II. Series.
GV865.P323M37 1998
796.357'092—dc21
[B]
          97-21985
          CIP
          AC

ABOUT THE AUTHOR: Barbara Marvis has been a writer for twenty years. She is the author of
several books for young adults including the *Contemporary American Success Stories* series and
Tommy Nuñez: NBA Referee/Taking My Best Shot. She holds a B.S. degree in English and communica-
tions from West Chester State University and an M.Ed. in remedial reading from the University of
Delaware. She specializes in writing books for children that can be read on several reading levels. She
lives with her husband, Bob, and their five children in northern Maryland.

PHOTO CREDITS: cover: Jerry Wachter; p. 4 sketch by Barbara Tidman; pp. 6, 8, 10, 12, 13, 19 courtesy
Maria Palmeiro; pp. 14, 16, 17, 28 courtesy Leaf, Inc., Topps, Score, and Fleer Corp.; p. 21 courtesy
Rafael and Lynne Palmeiro; p. 23 Jerry Wachter; p. 24 courtesy Baltimore Orioles; p. 25 Bettmann; p. 26
courtesy Baltimore Orioles; p. 28 courtesy Rafael and Lynne Palmeiro; p. 29 Globe Photos; p. 30 courtesy
Maria Palmeiro; p. 31 courtesy Rafael and Lynne Palmeiro

ACKNOWLEDGMENTS: The following story is an authorized biography. It is based on the author's
personal interviews with Rafael Palmeiro and his agent, Fernando Cuza. It has been thoroughly
researched, checked for accuracy, and approved by Rafael Palmeiro. To the best of our knowledge, it
represents a true story. Our sincerest appreciation goes to Rafael Palmeiro and his wife, Lynne; Maria
and José Palmeiro, and Fernando Cuza for supplying us with details and photographs for this biography.

15.95
8/25/98
DS

Table of Contents

Chapter 1
Young Rafael

Rafael Corrales Palmeiro was born on September 24, 1964, in Havana, Cuba. He was the second son born to Maria Corrales and José Palmeiro. He has an older brother, Rick, and a younger brother, André (Andy). He also has a half-brother, José Jr.

In Cuba, Rafael's father owned a concession stand. The family always had everything they needed. In 1959, all that changed when Fidel Castro took over as

In Cuba, the Palmeiros always had everything they needed.

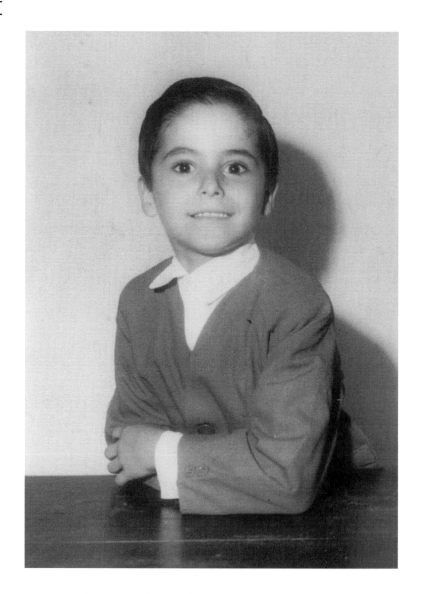

Rafael at four years old, taken in Cuba

President of Cuba. Castro took private businesses like the one José Palmeiro had and gave them to the government. A private citizen could no longer own a business.

Many people wanted to leave Cuba when Castro took over. They did not feel they had any freedom with Castro in control. Lots of people were able to leave the country in 1960 and 1961. Then Castro stopped letting people leave. The Palmeiro family was stuck in Cuba.

Some families tried to escape Cuba in boats. Not everyone made it. The Palmeiros decided to apply to the government to leave legally. It took until 1971 for Castro to allow them to go. But they had to leave all their belongings behind. They were not permitted to take anything with them. Not only did the Palmeiros lose all their money and possessions, but they had to leave José Jr. behind, too. Because José Jr.

The Palmeiros left Cuba in 1971. They were not allowed to take anything with them.

was of military age, Castro would not let him go with the rest of his family.

Mr. Palmeiro moved his family to safety in Miami, Florida. He got a job in the construction business. Rafael had started first grade in Cuba. He continued first grade in Miami. Rafael spoke only Spanish

Rafael, on right, at age 7, with Rick (left), age 8, and André (center), age 4

when he came to the United States. The school put him in a special class where the teachers spoke Spanish. Little by little, he learned English. It was hard.

"I hated school when I first came here," remembers Rafael. "I couldn't speak to anyone. I didn't know what anyone was talking about. When my mother would come to wake me in the morning, I would pretend I didn't hear her. She'd come back several times, trying to get me out of bed. I cried every day.

"After a few years, when I finally learned the language, then things were fun. I could finally speak to other people and I had friends at school."

"I hated school when I first came here. I couldn't speak to anyone. I didn't know what anyone was talking about."

Chapter 2
Early Love of Baseball

Even though the English language gave him difficulty, Rafael did well in school. "My favorite subject was always math," he says. But his favorite activity in school was sports. "I always loved to play sports in school, and by the time I was nine or ten, I knew I loved baseball most of all. When people would ask me what I wanted to be when I grew up, I would tell them, 'A baseball player.' Everyone thought that was cute. But as I got

"I always loved to play sports in school."

older, people would tell me that playing baseball was just a dream. My father told me I had better think of a real career. But I was always certain I'd have a baseball career."

In junior high school, Rafael played on a softball team and competed in tournaments throughout Miami. At Miami Jackson High School, he played on the school's baseball team in tenth through twelfth grades. He graduated from high school in 1982.

1981, playing ball for Miami Jackson High

"If you play sports well in high school, the colleges send people around to see you play," recalls

Rafael. He was offered a full scholarship to play baseball at Mississippi State University in Starkville, Mississippi. Rafael was also offered the chance to play professional ball right out of high school. He was selected by the New York Mets. But Rafael decided it was not the right time to sign. He needed some college experience first.

"My college years were lots of fun. Baseball was everything to me. There were thirty-five or

Rafael and his father built a dugout for Coral Gables High School in Florida.

forty players at my college that I hung around with. I was an all-American two years running at Mississippi State."

This 1988 baseball card shows Rafael in his Cubs uniform, ready to play.

Rafael never did get to finish his college degree, however. At the end of his junior year, he was drafted by the Chicago Cubs as a first-round pick. He decided then was the right time to sign. He was sure that he had what it took to make it in the major leagues. On June 11, 1985, Rafael was signed as a first-round amateur draft selection by scout Earl Winn.

Chapter 3
The Chicago Cubs

Like most ballplayers, Rafael had to start in the minor leagues. Minor-league players do not make very much money. Many times, they have to share apartments with the other players. This helps them stretch their money. But Rafael was engaged to Lynne Walden, and they wanted a place of their own. Rafael and Lynne had met in college. They were married in December 1985. It was difficult to make ends meet on his small salary.

Like most ballplayers, Rafael had to start in the minor leagues.

In the minor leagues, the ball clubs hope to train players they can one day use on their major-league teams. Players accept very small salaries in the minors because they hope they will someday make a lot of money in the major leagues. Only a small number of minor-league players ever make it to the major leagues and stay there, however. Most of the players are young. They all have hopes of becoming baseball stars one day. Rafael knew that a lot of his teammates had talent, too. He knew that he would have to play the best of all to outshine the others.

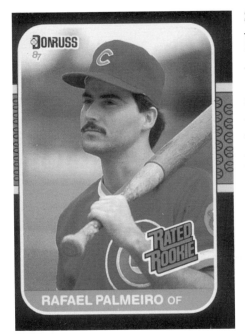

Rafael's rookie card, after his first season with the Cubs.

In the minor leagues, there are four levels of play. The rookie league plays about sixty games each summer. A-ball, double-A, and triple-A teams play 144 games each season. Rafael began his baseball career in Peoria, Illinois, playing on the Cubs' A-ball team.

Rafael played seventy-three games in Peoria and finished the season with a batting average of .297. He hit five home runs in his rookie season, with fifty-one runs batted in (RBIs). Then he was promoted to the double-A team in Pittsfield for the 1986 season. He was the most valuable player (MVP) of the Eastern league that season.

Rafael played hard at every game. He wanted to be better than everyone else. He was not very happy when he did not do well.

1988 Topps card of Rafael. It shows he led the Eastern League with 156 hits, 95 RBIs and 225 total bases in 1986.

His return to the minor leagues was short. He was recalled by Chicago later that season.

In September 1986, Rafael was called up to Chicago. "I was so excited," remembers Rafael. "This was everything I had been working for." Rafael played twenty-two games for the Cubs that season.

But when spring training began for the 1987 season, Rafael was sent back to triple-A in Iowa. He was disappointed that he didn't start with the Cubs that year. His return to the minor leagues was short, however. He was recalled by Chicago later that season. He has never since played another minor-league game. In 1987, Rafael had the highest batting average of all the National League rookies. He finally had a real baseball career.

Rafael did well his next year in the majors. It was a very exciting time for him. He had a twenty-game hitting streak. He played in

152 games that year and finished the season batting .307. Then the fans selected him to play on the National League All-Star Team. After the 1988 season, Rafael was honored again. He was chosen to go to Japan to play for the United States on the Major League All-Star Team.

From left to right: Fern Cuza (Rafael's agent), Rafael's father, José, brother Rick, Rafael, Miguel Gallego, and brother, Andy

Chapter 4
The Texas Rangers

Even though Rafael had been playing very well, the Cubs traded him to the Rangers.

Even though Rafael had been playing very well, on December 5, 1988, the Chicago Cubs traded him to the Texas Rangers. Lynne and Rafael moved to Texas and bought their first house. "I liked playing for the Rangers," says Rafael. "I had a lot of friends and good teammates. The ballpark was real convenient to my home. It was only two minutes away. I was very happy there."

Rafael played for the Rangers for the next five years. He was their first baseman or a designated hitter. In 1990, Rafael led the league with 191 hits in 154 games. His batting average of .319 put him third in the league. That year he was named the Texas Rangers' MVP. In 1991, he hit 49 doubles and scored 115 runs to create a new team record.

Rafael is training son, Patrick, for the major leagues.

In 1993, Rafael led his league with 124 runs in 160 games. He proved many times that he was a top player. But he was not happy when the Rangers made him their offer for the next season. "It didn't seem like they cared about me," says Rafael. It was time for Rafael to move on. He turned down their offer.

Chapter 5
The Baltimore Orioles

In 1993, Rafael became a free agent. He accepted an offer to play for Baltimore.

On October 25, 1993, Rafael became a free agent. This meant that he could listen to offers from any ball club. In December 1993, he decided to go play for the Baltimore Orioles. They had offered him a good contract to come play for them.

On opening day in Baltimore in April 1994, Rafael received big cheers from the crowd when he was introduced. Then, in the seventh inning against the Kansas City

Royals, Rafael hit a home run. All his fans were standing and cheering. Rafael circled the bases, but when he got home, the crowd was still cheering. Rafael had to go to the top steps of the dugout and wave his cap at the crowd. They finally stopped cheering. "I've never had fans that made me feel so

Rafael (on right) with Roberto Alomar (left) and Cal Ripken Jr. (center) at spring training, 1996

This 1994 team picture was taken the first year Rafael played for Baltimore.

special," said Rafael. "That made me want to play my best for them."

Rafael still finds baseball very exciting. He loves it when he plays well. He was proud to be a part of the game when his Oriole teammate Cal Ripken Jr. broke Lou Gehrig's record for playing the most games in a row. President Bill Clinton came to the game that night, and Rafael brought his oldest son, Patrick, to meet him. When

Rafael tips his cap to his roaring fans.

Cal Ripken Jr, Rafael's teammate on the Orioles, broke Lou Gehrig's consecutive game record on September 7, 1995.

President Clinton went to sign his name on Patrick's cap, Patrick yelled, "No! That's Mommy's hat."

There was more history made in 1996. On April 30, the Orioles and the Yankees broke the major league record for the longest nine-inning game. They played for four hours and twenty-one minutes. In September 1996, Rafael watched his teammate Eddie Murray hit his 500th home run.

"It takes a lot of hard work to be a good hitter in the majors," says Rafael. ". . . My approach to hitting is this: I'm going to drive the ball. I don't choke up with two strikes. It's going to cost me points on my batting average, but as long as I'm producing for the team, that's okay."

And Rafael surely did produce results for the Orioles. In 1996, he hit 39 home runs and 142 RBIs. He helped his team win the wild card spot in the American League playoffs.

This was the first time the Orioles had made it to the playoffs in thirteen years. They had to face the powerful Cleveland Indians, who had won their Central Division championship. The Orioles won the series against the Indians. But then they had to face the mighty New York Yankees, who had beaten them in many games during the season.

Game one of the best-of-seven series began in Yankee Stadium on October 10, 1996. It was the strangest of all the games played that season. It started off well. Brady Anderson hit a home run in the third inning. Rafael hit a home

1996 was the first time the Orioles had made it to the playoffs in thirteen years.

run in the fourth inning to give the Orioles a 3-2 lead. The Orioles got another run in the sixth to make the

score 4-2. Then the Yankees got another run in the seventh. The Orioles' lead was cut to one

Before and after many games, Rafael is mobbed for autographs by his fans.

run. Then came the strangest eighth inning. There was one out. The Yankee shortstop, Derek Jeter, hit a fly ball to right field. Oriole rightfielder Tony Tarasco had his sights on the ball. He backed up to the right field wall and raised his glove.

Then, ZOOP! The ball disappeared like magic. Tony stood

there empty-handed. Umpire Rich Garcia signaled a home run for Derek Jeter. But where was the ball? Twelve-year-old Jeff Maier, a Yankee fan, had stuck his glove out over the wall and brought the ball into the stands. The umpire did not see the interference.

The Oriole players were angry. They protested the umpire's call. Manager Davey Johnson argued for ten minutes. He was thrown out of the game. Yankee fans gave Jeff Maier high fives. Derek Jeter circled the bases and tied the score.

Jeff Maier shows where the ball went.

The game then went into extra innings. The Yankees won in the eleventh inning. The Orioles felt they should have won that game. They vowed to get even.

The Orioles gave it their best shot, but the New York Yankees went on to win the series. The Yankees went to the World Series and beat the Atlanta Braves, too.

When Rafael is not playing baseball, he enjoys spending time

Rafael with his mother and brothers, Rick and Andy

with his family. Rafael and Lynne have two sons: Patrick, born in 1990, and Preston, born in 1995. "I'm living my dream right now," says Rafael. "Baltimore is a wonderful team to play for, and I hope to end my career, many years from now, right here in Baltimore."

The Palmeiro family poses in Oriole uniforms: left to right, rear: Rafael, wife, Lynne, son Preston (on lap left) and son Patrick

Chronology

- Born September 24, 1964, in Havana, Cuba; mother: Maria Corrales; father: José Palmeiro
- Family left Cuba in 1971
- Grew up in Miami, Florida
- 1982, graduated from Miami Jackson High School
- 1982–1985 attended Mississippi State University
- June 11, 1985, signed with Chicago Cubs
- December 1985, married Lynne Walden
- 1988, ranked second in the National League in batting; had twenty-game hitting streak; selected to play on the National League All-Star team
- 1989, played for Texas Rangers; 1990, was Texas Rangers' MVP
- 1993, signed contract to play for the Baltimore Orioles
- Currently: married to Lynne Walden; they have two sons: Patrick and Preston; they live in both Texas and in Baltimore, Maryland

Index